The Ultimate Brownie Book

40 Delicious Recipes for Cream
Cheese Delights and More

Norma Hunter

THIS BOOK BELONGS TO:

_____

_____

Thanks ever so much to each of my cherished readers for investing the time to read this book!

I know you could have picked from many other books, but you chose this one. So, a big thanks for reading all the way to the end. If you enjoyed this book or received value from it, I'd like to ask you for a favor. Please take a few minutes to **post an honest and heartfelt review on** Amazon.com. Your support does make a difference and helps to benefit other people.

Thanks!

License Notes

No part of this Book can be reproduced in any form or by any means including print, electronic, scanning or photocopying unless prior permission is granted by the author.

All ideas, suggestions and guidelines mentioned here are written for informative purposes. While the author has taken every possible step to ensure accuracy, all readers are advised to follow information at their own risk. The author cannot be held responsible for personal and/or commercial damages in case of misinterpreting and misunderstanding any part of this Book

Table of Contents

Summary

The Universal Love for Brownies: The universal love for brownies is a phenomenon that transcends cultural boundaries and brings people together in a shared appreciation for this delectable dessert. Brownies, with their rich chocolate flavor and fudgy texture, have become a beloved treat worldwide.

One of the reasons for the universal love for brownies is their versatility. Brownies can be enjoyed in various forms, from classic plain chocolate brownies to those infused with nuts, caramel, or even fruits. This versatility allows for endless possibilities and caters to different taste preferences, ensuring that there is a brownie for everyone.

Furthermore, brownies are incredibly easy to make, making them accessible to both experienced bakers and novices alike. With just a few simple ingredients and a quick baking time, anyone can whip up a batch of brownies to satisfy their sweet tooth. This accessibility has contributed to the widespread popularity of brownies, as they can be enjoyed by people of all ages and skill levels.

Another factor that contributes to the universal love for brownies is their nostalgic appeal. Many people have fond memories of baking or enjoying brownies with loved ones, whether it be during childhood or at family gatherings. The smell of freshly baked brownies wafting through the kitchen can evoke feelings of warmth and comfort, making them a go-to dessert for many.

Additionally, brownies have become a staple in many cultures and cuisines around the world. While they may have originated in the United States, brownies have found their way into the hearts and stomachs of people from all corners of the globe. Whether it's a gooey chocolate brownie in the United States, a dense and fudgy brownie in Europe, or a chewy and nutty brownie in Asia, each culture has put its own unique twist on this beloved dessert.

The universal love for brownies is also evident in the numerous variations and adaptations that have been created over the years. From brownie sundaes to brownie cheesecakes, the possibilities for incorporating brownies into other desserts are endless. This creativity and innovation have only further fueled the adoration for brownies, as people continue to experiment with new and exciting ways to enjoy this timeless treat.

In conclusion, the universal love for brownies can be attributed to their versatility, accessibility, nostalgic appeal, cultural significance, and the endless possibilities for variation. Whether enjoyed plain or dressed up with additional ingredients, brownies have a way of bringing people together and satisfying their sweet cravings.

The Exciting World of Brownie Variations: The exciting world of brownie variations is a delightful and mouthwatering journey that takes us beyond the traditional chocolate brownie. While the classic chocolate brownie is undeniably delicious, there is a whole universe of flavors and textures waiting to be explored.

One of the most popular variations is the fudgy brownie. These brownies are dense and moist, with a rich and intense chocolate flavor. They are often made with a higher ratio of chocolate to flour, resulting in a gooey and indulgent treat. Fudgy brownies are perfect for those who prefer a more decadent and sinful dessert experience.

On the other end of the spectrum, we have the cakey brownie. These brownies have a lighter and fluffier texture, resembling a traditional cake. They are often made with a higher ratio of flour to chocolate, resulting in a more cake-like consistency. Cakey brownies are perfect for those who enjoy a lighter and less dense dessert option.

For those who love a little crunch in their brownies, there are the chewy brownies. These brownies have a slightly crispy exterior and a chewy interior, providing a delightful contrast in textures. They are often made with a combination of melted chocolate and cocoa powder, resulting in a perfect balance of flavors. Chewy brownies are perfect for those who enjoy a bit of texture in their desserts.

If you're feeling adventurous, you can also explore the world of flavored brownies. From mint chocolate brownies to peanut butter swirl brownies, the possibilities are endless. These variations add an extra layer of complexity and excitement to the traditional brownie recipe.

They are perfect for those who want to experiment with different flavors and surprise their taste buds.

Furthermore, brownies can also be customized to cater to specific dietary needs. For those who follow a gluten-free diet, there are numerous recipes that use alternative flours such as almond flour or coconut flour. Vegan brownies can be made using ingredients like applesauce or flaxseed as egg substitutes. These variations ensure that everyone can enjoy the deliciousness of brownies, regardless of their dietary restrictions.

In conclusion, the exciting world of brownie variations offers a wide range of flavors, textures, and customization options. Whether you prefer a fudgy, cakey, or chewy brownie, or if you want to explore unique flavors and cater to specific dietary needs, there is a brownie variation out there for you.

Purpose and Structure of Brownies Book: The purpose of the book Brownies is to entertain and engage readers with a heartwarming and relatable story. It aims to explore themes of friendship, loyalty, and the challenges of growing up. The structure of the book is carefully crafted to captivate readers and keep them hooked from beginning to end.

The book starts by introducing the main characters, a group of young girls who are part of a Brownie troop. The author takes the time to establish each character's unique personality and background, allowing readers to form a connection with them. This helps to create a sense of familiarity and investment in the story.

As the plot unfolds, the book delves into the girls' adventures and misadventures as they navigate the ups and downs of their friendship. The author skillfully weaves in moments of humor, drama, and emotion, ensuring that readers are constantly engaged and eager to find out what happens next.

The structure of the book is divided into chapters, each focusing on a different event or aspect of the girls' lives. This allows for a sense of progression and development in the story, as readers witness the characters' growth and maturation. The chapters are carefully paced, with a balance of action and reflection, ensuring that readers are never overwhelmed or bored.

Throughout the book, the author incorporates vivid descriptions and sensory details, bringing the story to life and allowing readers to fully immerse themselves in the world of the Brownies. This attention to detail helps to create a rich and vibrant reading experience.

In addition to the main plotline, the book also explores important themes such as diversity, acceptance, and the power of teamwork. The author uses the girls' experiences and interactions to highlight these themes, encouraging readers to reflect on their own lives and relationships.

The book concludes with a satisfying resolution, tying up loose ends and leaving readers with a sense of closure. The author ensures that the characters' journeys are complete, while still leaving room for readers to imagine their future adventures.

Overall, the purpose and structure of the book Brownies work together to create a compelling and enjoyable reading experience. The author's attention to detail, engaging plot, and relatable characters make it a book that readers of all ages can appreciate and enjoy.

Utilizing This Cookbook to Create Brownie Perfection:

If you're a fan of brownies, then you're in luck! With the help of this cookbook, you can create brownie perfection right in your own kitchen. Whether you prefer fudgy, gooey brownies or a more cake-like texture, this cookbook has got you covered.

To start off, the cookbook provides a variety of brownie recipes to suit every taste. From classic chocolate brownies to unique flavors like salted caramel or peanut butter swirl, there's something for everyone. Each recipe is carefully crafted to ensure the perfect balance of flavors and textures, resulting in a truly decadent treat.

One of the key features of this cookbook is its detailed instructions. Each recipe is accompanied by step-by-step directions, making it easy for even novice bakers to follow along. The instructions are clear and concise, leaving no room for confusion or error. Additionally, the cookbook includes helpful tips and tricks to ensure success with each batch of brownies.

Another standout feature of this cookbook is its emphasis on quality ingredients. The recipes call for high-quality chocolate, butter, and other essential ingredients, ensuring that the end result is nothing short of perfection. The cookbook also provides recommendations for specific brands or types of ingredients to use, further enhancing the overall taste and texture of the brownies.

In addition to the recipes themselves, this cookbook also offers variations and customization options. Whether you want to add nuts, chocolate chips, or even a swirl of cream cheese, the cookbook provides suggestions and guidelines for adapting the recipes to suit your preferences. This allows you to get creative and experiment with different flavors and textures, making each batch of brownies truly unique.

Furthermore, the cookbook includes helpful troubleshooting tips. Baking can sometimes be a finicky process, and even the most experienced bakers can encounter issues along the way. This cookbook addresses common problems that may arise, such as undercooked centers or dry edges, and provides solutions to ensure that your brownies turn out perfectly every time.

Lastly, this cookbook offers a range of serving suggestions and presentation ideas. After all, presentation is just as important as taste when it comes to creating brownie perfection. The cookbook provides suggestions for garnishes, sauces, and even ice cream pairings to elevate your brownies to the next level.

In conclusion, if you're looking to create brownie perfection, look no further than this cookbook. With its variety of recipes, detailed instructions, emphasis on quality ingredients,

Understanding the Basics of Brownie Baking: Brownie baking is a popular and delicious activity that many people enjoy. Whether you are a beginner or an experienced baker, it is important to understand the basics of brownie baking in order to achieve the perfect batch every time.

First and foremost, it is crucial to gather all the necessary ingredients before starting the baking process. The main ingredients for brownies typically include flour, sugar, butter, eggs, and chocolate. It is important to use high-quality ingredients to ensure the best flavor and texture in your brownies.

Next, it is important to preheat your oven to the correct temperature. Most brownie recipes call for an oven temperature of around 350 degrees Fahrenheit (175 degrees Celsius). Preheating the oven ensures that the brownies bake evenly and have a nice, crispy top.

Once your oven is preheated, it is time to prepare the brownie batter. This involves mixing the dry ingredients (flour, sugar, and cocoa powder) together in one bowl, and the wet ingredients (butter and eggs) in another bowl. It is important to mix the wet and dry ingredients separately before combining them together. This ensures that the ingredients are evenly distributed throughout the batter.

When combining the wet and dry ingredients, it is important to mix them together gently. Overmixing can lead to tough and dense brownies. Use a spatula or wooden spoon to fold the ingredients together until just combined.

Once the batter is mixed, it is time to add any additional ingredients or mix-ins. This is where you can get creative and add things like nuts, chocolate chips, or even a swirl of caramel. These additions can add extra flavor and texture to your brownies.

After the batter is prepared, it is time to pour it into a greased baking pan. The size of the pan will depend on the desired thickness of your brownies. A 9x9 inch (23x23 cm) pan is a common size for brownies. Make sure to spread the batter evenly in the pan to ensure even baking.

Now it is time to bake the brownies in the preheated oven. The baking time will vary depending on the recipe and the size of the pan. It is important to keep an eye on the brownies and check for doneness by inserting a toothpick into the center. If it comes out with a few moist crumbs, the brownies are done. Be careful not to overbake them, as this can result in dry and crumb.

Essential Ingredients and Baking Equipment: To successfully bake any recipe, it is crucial to have the essential ingredients and baking equipment on hand. These components play a vital role in achieving the desired outcome of your baked goods. Whether you are a seasoned baker or a novice in the kitchen, understanding the importance of these elements will greatly enhance your baking experience.

First and foremost, let's delve into the essential ingredients required for baking. Flour is the foundation of most baked goods, providing structure and texture. There are various types of flour available, such as all-purpose flour, bread flour, and cake flour, each with its own unique properties. It is important to choose the right type of flour based on the recipe you are following.

Another crucial ingredient is sugar, which not only adds sweetness but also aids in browning and caramelization. Granulated sugar is the most commonly used type, but there are alternatives like brown sugar, powdered sugar, and even natural sweeteners like honey or maple syrup. The choice of sugar will depend on the desired flavor and texture of your baked goods.

Leavening agents, such as baking powder and baking soda, are essential for creating light and airy baked goods. Baking powder is a combination of baking soda, cream of tartar, and a moisture-absorbing agent. It is used in recipes that require a quick rise, such as cakes and muffins. Baking soda, on the other hand, requires an acidic ingredient like buttermilk or vinegar to activate its leavening properties. It is commonly used in recipes like cookies and quick breads.

Fats, such as butter, oil, or shortening, are crucial for adding moisture and richness to baked goods. Butter is a popular choice for its flavor, while oil and shortening are preferred for their ability to create a tender texture. The choice of fat will depend on the specific recipe and personal preference.

Eggs are another essential ingredient in baking, providing structure, moisture, and richness. They act as a binding agent and help emulsify the other ingredients. In some recipes, eggs can be substituted with alternatives like applesauce, mashed bananas, or yogurt for dietary restrictions or personal preference.

Now that we have covered the essential ingredients, let's move on to the baking equipment necessary for successful baking. A good quality set of measuring cups and spoons is essential for accurately measuring ingredients. Baking is a science, and precise measurements are crucial for achieving consistent results.

Tips and Techniques for Baking Perfect Brownies Every Time:

Baking brownies can be a delightful and rewarding experience, especially when you achieve that perfect balance of fudgy and chewy texture with a rich chocolate flavor. However, it can also be a bit tricky to get them just right. To help you master the art of baking perfect brownies every time, here are some tips and techniques to keep in mind.

1. Choose the Right Recipe: The first step to baking perfect brownies is selecting a reliable and well-tested recipe. Look for recipes that have been reviewed and rated positively by other bakers. It's also important to consider the type of brownie you prefer - whether it's fudgy, cakey, or somewhere in between. Different recipes will yield different results, so choose one that aligns with your desired texture.

2. Use High-Quality Ingredients: The quality of your ingredients can greatly impact the final outcome of your brownies. Opt for high-quality chocolate, cocoa powder, and vanilla extract to enhance the flavor. Using unsalted butter instead of margarine or shortening will also contribute to a richer taste. Additionally, using fresh eggs and measuring ingredients accurately will ensure consistent results.

3. Prepare the Pan Properly: To prevent your brownies from sticking to the pan, it's crucial to prepare it properly. Grease the pan with butter or cooking spray, and then line it with parchment paper. This will make it easier to remove the brownies once they're baked, ensuring they come out in perfect squares.

4. Don't Overmix the Batter: When it comes to mixing the batter, less is more. Overmixing can lead to tough and dense brownies. Mix the ingredients until they are just combined, and avoid using a mixer if possible. A wooden spoon or spatula is usually sufficient for this task.

5. Control the Baking Time and Temperature: The baking time and temperature are critical factors in achieving the perfect brownie texture. Follow the recipe instructions carefully, but keep in mind that every oven is different. Start checking for doneness a few minutes before the recommended time. Insert a toothpick into the center of the brownies - if it comes out with a few moist crumbs, they are done. If the toothpick comes out with wet batter, they need more time. Be cautious not to overbake, as this can result in dry brownies.

Customizing and Experimenting with Brownie Recipes: Customizing and experimenting with brownie recipes can be a fun and exciting way to add your own personal touch to this classic dessert. Brownies are loved by many for their rich and fudgy texture, and by customizing the recipe, you can create a unique flavor profile that suits your taste preferences.

One way to customize a brownie recipe is by adding different types of chocolate. While traditional brownie recipes call for semi-sweet or dark chocolate, you can experiment with using milk chocolate, white chocolate, or even a combination of different chocolates. Each type of chocolate will bring its own distinct flavor and sweetness to the brownies, allowing you to create a variety of taste experiences.

In addition to experimenting with different types of chocolate, you can also add various mix-ins to your brownie batter. Popular mix-ins include nuts, such as walnuts or pecans, which add a crunchy texture and a nutty flavor to the brownies. You can also try adding dried fruits, like cherries or cranberries, for a burst of sweetness and tanginess. For those who enjoy a bit of indulgence, you can even incorporate chunks of your favorite candy bars or cookies into the batter.

Furthermore, you can customize the texture of your brownies by adjusting the baking time and temperature. If you prefer a gooey and fudgy brownie, you can bake them for a shorter amount of time at a lower temperature. On the other hand, if you prefer a cake-like texture, you can bake them for a longer time at a higher temperature. By experimenting with different baking times and temperatures, you can find the perfect balance between a soft and chewy brownie or a light and fluffy one.

Another way to customize your brownie recipe is by adding different flavorings and spices. For example, you can add a teaspoon of instant coffee or espresso powder to enhance the chocolate flavor. You can also incorporate a teaspoon of vanilla extract or almond extract to add a subtle hint of sweetness. Additionally, spices like cinnamon or chili powder can add a unique and unexpected twist to your brownies.

Finally, you can experiment with different toppings to elevate the presentation and taste of your brownies. A classic option is to dust the top of the brownies with powdered sugar or cocoa powder. You can also drizzle melted chocolate or caramel sauce over the brownies for an extra touch of decadence. For a refreshing twist, you can top your brownies with a scoop of ice cream or a dollop

The Joy of Baking Traditional Brownies: Baking traditional brownies is a delightful experience that brings joy to both the baker and those who get to enjoy the delicious end result. The process of making these classic treats involves a few simple steps, but the outcome is a rich and fudgy dessert that is sure to satisfy any sweet tooth.

To begin, gather all the necessary ingredients. Traditional brownies typically call for butter, sugar, eggs, vanilla extract, flour, cocoa powder, and a pinch of salt. It's important to use high-quality ingredients to ensure the best flavor and texture in your brownies.

Next, preheat your oven to the recommended temperature, usually around 350 degrees Fahrenheit. While the oven is heating up, melt the butter in a saucepan over low heat. Once the butter has melted, remove it from the heat and stir in the sugar until well combined. This step helps to create a smooth and creamy base for the brownies.

In a separate bowl, beat the eggs and vanilla extract together until they are well mixed. Slowly add the egg mixture to the butter and sugar mixture, stirring constantly. This helps to incorporate air into the batter, resulting in a lighter and fluffier brownie.

In another bowl, sift together the flour, cocoa powder, and salt. Sifting the dry ingredients helps to remove any lumps and ensures an even distribution of the cocoa powder throughout the batter. Gradually add the dry ingredients to the wet ingredients, stirring gently until just combined. Be careful not to overmix, as this can lead to a dense and tough brownie.

Once the batter is ready, pour it into a greased baking dish. The size of the dish will depend on how thick you want your brownies to be. A 9x9-inch square pan is a common choice, but you can also use a rectangular pan or even a round cake pan if desired.

Place the baking dish in the preheated oven and bake for the recommended time, usually around 25-30 minutes. Keep a close eye on the brownies towards the end of the baking time to ensure they don't overcook. The brownies are done when a toothpick inserted into the center comes out with a few moist crumbs clinging to it. Remember that the brownies will continue to cook slightly as they cool, so it's better to slightly underbake them than to overbake them.

The Richness and Flavor of Cream Cheese Variations for Brownies: When it comes to adding richness and flavor to brownies, cream cheese variations are a game-changer. Cream cheese not only enhances the texture of the brownies but also adds a creamy and tangy element that takes the taste to a whole new level.

One popular cream cheese variation for brownies is the classic cream cheese swirl. This involves swirling a mixture of cream cheese, sugar, and vanilla into the brownie batter before baking. As the brownies bake, the cream cheese mixture creates a beautiful marbled effect, resulting in a visually appealing treat. The cream cheese swirl adds a velvety smoothness to the brownies and balances out the sweetness with its tangy flavor.

Another delicious cream cheese variation for brownies is the cream cheese frosting. This involves spreading a layer of cream cheese frosting on top of the baked brownies. The frosting adds a luscious and creamy texture to the brownies, making them even more indulgent. The tanginess of the cream cheese complements the rich chocolate flavor of the brownies, creating a perfect harmony of tastes.

For those who prefer a more intense cream cheese flavor, there is the option of incorporating cream cheese into the brownie batter itself. This can be done by adding softened cream cheese to the batter along with the other ingredients. The cream cheese not only adds a distinct flavor but also contributes to the moistness and fudginess of the brownies. The result is a decadent treat with a melt-in-your-mouth texture and a pronounced cream cheese taste.

Cream cheese variations for brownies also offer endless possibilities for customization. For example, you can experiment with different flavors by adding ingredients such as cocoa powder, espresso powder, or even fruit purees to the cream cheese mixture. This allows you to create unique and personalized brownies that cater to your taste preferences.

In conclusion, cream cheese variations are a fantastic way to elevate the richness and flavor of brownies. Whether it's through a marbled cream cheese swirl, a creamy frosting, or incorporating cream cheese into the batter, these variations add a delightful tanginess and creaminess to the brownies. With the ability to customize and experiment with different flavors, cream cheese variations for brownies are sure to satisfy any sweet tooth and leave you craving for more.

Elevating Brownies with Unique Flavors and Ingredients:

When it comes to indulging in a sweet treat, brownies are a classic choice that never disappoints. However, if you're looking to take your brownie experience to the next level, why not try elevating them with unique flavors and ingredients? By experimenting with different combinations, you can create a truly extraordinary brownie that will leave your taste buds craving for more.

One way to elevate your brownies is by incorporating unique flavors into the batter. Instead of sticking to the traditional chocolate base, consider adding a hint of espresso for a rich and bold taste. The coffee undertones will complement the chocolate perfectly, creating a decadent and sophisticated flavor profile. Alternatively, you can infuse your brownies with a touch of citrus by adding orange or lemon zest. The zesty notes will add a refreshing twist to the dense and fudgy texture of the brownies, making them a delightful treat for any occasion.

In addition to experimenting with flavors, you can also elevate your brownies by incorporating unique ingredients. For example, adding a swirl of creamy peanut butter to the batter will create a delightful contrast of flavors and textures. The smooth and nutty peanut butter will complement the rich chocolate, resulting in a heavenly combination that will satisfy any sweet tooth. Another option is to mix in chunks of your favorite candy or nuts for an added crunch and burst of flavor. Whether it's crushed Oreos, chopped almonds, or even a sprinkle of sea salt, these additions will take your brownies to a whole new level of deliciousness.

Furthermore, you can elevate your brownies by exploring different toppings and garnishes. Instead of simply dusting them with powdered sugar, consider drizzling them with a homemade caramel sauce or a velvety ganache. The sticky sweetness of the caramel or the smooth richness of the ganache will add an extra layer of indulgence to your brownies. Additionally, you can top them with a scoop of your favorite ice cream or a dollop of whipped cream for a truly decadent dessert experience.

In conclusion, elevating brownies with unique flavors and ingredients is a surefire way to enhance your sweet tooth satisfaction. By experimenting with different combinations, you can create a brownie that is truly extraordinary and unforgettable. So, the next time you're craving a delicious treat, don't settle for ordinary brownies. Instead, let your creativity run wild and elevate your brownie game to new heights.

Brownies

Bourbon Pecan Brownies with Bacon

One for the man in your life, these naughty brownies are topped with crispy bacon bits and flavored with a good glug of bourbon.

Portions: 12-14

Prep Time: 10mins

Cooking Time: 50mins

Total Time: 1hour

Ingredients:

- Nonstick spray
- 8 ounces semisweet choc chips
- 2 ounces bitter choc chips
- ½ cup +2 tbsp. salted butter

- ½ pound bacon rashers (cooked, chopped, 3 tbsp. bacon cooking fat reserved)
- 1 cup white sugar
- ½ cup brown sugar
- 4 eggs
- 3 tbsp. bourbon
- 1 tsp kosher salt
- 1½ cups all-purpose flour
- ½ cup cocoa powder (unsweetened)
- ½ cup pecans (chopped)

Directions:

1. Preheat the main oven to 350 degrees F. Line a 9" square baking tin with parchment and spritz with nonstick spray.

2. Melt together the choc chips and butter using a microwave, stir until silky and transfer to a mixing bowl along with the bacon fat and sugars. Beat until combined.

3. Add the eggs, bourbon, and salt. Beat again. Fold in the flour and cocoa powder.

4. Pour the batter into the tin. Sprinkle with the chopped bacon and pecans.

5. Place in the oven and bake for 50 minutes. Allow to cool before slicing and serving.

Caffeine Lover's Espresso Oatmeal Brownies

Why not start the day with a square of these delicious brownies that combine our two favorite breakfast items; coffee and oatmeal!?

Portions: 12

Prep Time: 10mins

Cooking Time: 35mins

Total Time: 45mins

Ingredients:

- Butter (for greasing)
- 1 cup oats
- ¼ tsp bicarb of soda
- ½ tsp baking powder
- ½ tsp kosher salt

- ⅔ cup dark chocolate (chopped)
- ½ cup unsalted butter (chilled, cubed)
- ¼ cup freshly brewed espresso (cooled)
- 3½ ounces light brown sugar
- 1 tsp vanilla essence
- 3 medium eggs

Directions:

1. Preheat the main oven to 360 degrees F. Grease an 8" square baking tin and line.

2. Add the oats to a food processor and blitz until powdery.

3. Transfer the oats to a mixing bowl along with the bicarb of soda, baking powder, and kosher salt. Set aside for a moment.

4. Melt together the dark chocolate and butter in a saucepan over moderately low heat. Stir until silky smooth.

5. Add the brewed espresso and sugar, stir while heating until the sugar dissolves.

6. Take off the heat and set aside to cool a little.

7. Stir in the vanilla essence, then the eggs one at a time until incorporated.

8. Add the set-aside flour mixture to the melted mixture a little at a time, mix until just combined.

9. Pour the batter into the baking tin and place in the oven. Bake for just over 25 minutes until set.

10. Allow to cool a little before slicing and serving warm.

Caramel Fudge Brownies

The one pot caramel fudge brownies will have you drooling as you whip them up.

Portions: 9

Prep Time: 10mins

Cooking Time: 55mins

Total Time: 1hour 5mins

Ingredients:

- ¾ cup salted butter
- 1 cup light brown sugar
- ¾ cup white sugar
- Yolk of 1 medium egg
- 3 medium eggs
- 1 tbsp. vanilla essence
- ½ tsp kosher salt
- ½ cup all-purpose flour

- 1 cup cocoa powder (unsweetened)
- 1 (9 ounce) bag mini chocolate caramel candies
- ¾ cup caramel sauce

Directions:

1. Preheat the main oven to 350 degrees F. Grease an 8" square baking tin and line with parchment.

2. Melt the butter in a large pot over moderate heat. Take off the heat and immediately whisk in the sugars.

3. Beat in the yolk and eggs, until incorporated, then the vanilla essence.

4. Fold in the kosher salt, flour and cocoa powder.

5. Fold in a cup of the chocolate caramel candies.

6. Pour the batter into the tin and dollop spoonfuls of caramel sauce on top. Swirl with a knife.

7. Sprinkle with the remaining candies.

8. Place in the oven and bake for just over 50 minutes.

9. Allow to cool before slicing.

Choc Chip Cookie Dough Brownies

Finally, our two favorite sweet treats come together to make these choc chip cookie dough brownies.

Portions: 9-12

Prep Time: 10mins

Cooking Time: 55mins

Total Time: 1hour 5mins

Ingredients:

Cookie Dough:

- 1 cup light brown sugar
- ¾ cup salted butter (softened)
- 1 tsp vanilla essence
- 1 medium egg
- 1½ cups all-purpose flour
- 1 tsp bicarb of soda
- 1 tsp kosher salt

- 1 cup semisweet choc chips
- 14 mini chocolate caramel filled candies

Brownie:

- 1 (2o ounce) box brownie mix

Directions:

1. Preheat the main oven to 350 degrees F. Line an 8" square baking tin with parchment.

2. Make the cookie dough. Beat together the brown sugar, butter, vanilla essence, and egg.

3. Fold in the flour, bicarb of soda and salt.

4. Stir in the choc chips and press the dough into the tin. Squish the candies between your fingers to 'smash' them, then scatter on top of the dough.

5. Prepare the brownie mix according to box instructions, using all extra ingredients called for.

6. Pour the batter over the cookie dough.

7. Put in the oven and bake for just under an hour.

8. Allow to cool before slicing and serving.

Coco Loco Brownies

Brownies can't get any better than this! Chocolate combined with cocoa powder and coconut milk has to be the best brownie ever!

Portions: 24

Prep Time: 20mins

Cooking Time: 45mins

Total Time: 1hour 35mins

Ingredients:

- Butter (for greasing)
- ½ cup salted butter
- 2 cups granulated sugar
- 2 cups semisweet choc chips
- 2 large eggs
- 1 tsp vanilla essence

- 1 cup canned coconut milk
- 1¼ cups cocoa powder
- 1 tsp baking powder
- 1 tsp salt
- 1½ cups all-purpose flour

Frosting:

- ½ cup butter (at room temperature)
- ⅓ cup coconut milk
- 1 tsp vanilla essence
- ⅓ cup cocoa powder
- 2-2½ cups confectioner's sugar

Directions:

1. Preheat the main oven to 350 degrees F. Lightly grease a 9x 13" dish.

2. In a saucepan over moderate heat, melt the butter.

3. Continue to cook, stir in the sugar followed by the choc chips for a couple of minutes, until melted. Do not boil.

4. Pour the butter/chocolate mixture into a stand mixer bowl. Beat in the eggs, vanilla, and coconut milk.

5. Combine the cocoa powder, baking powder, salt, and flour in a small bowl.

6. With the stand mixer running, add the flour mixture a little at a time to the coconut milk mixture until combined.

7. Pour the batter into the dish and place in the oven. Bake for approximately 40 minutes. Set aside to cool.

8. Prepare the frosting. In a bowl, whip the butter up. Add the coconut milk and vanilla essence, beat until combined.

9. Gradually, and a little at a time, mix in the cocoa powder.

10. Add the confectioner's sugar, a half a cup at a time, until the frosting has reached its desired spreadable consistency.

11. Spread the mixture over the cooled brownie, slice and enjoy.

Dark Chocolate Nutty Brownies

These sinfully rich brownies have chunks of crunchy roasted hazelnuts for a nutty coffee-time delight.

Portions: 9

Prep Time: 10mins

Cooking Time: 35mins

Total Time: 45mins

Ingredients:

- Nonstick spray
- 5 ounces semisweet choc chips

- 2 ounces bitter choc chips
- ½ cup unsalted butter
- 3 tbsp. cocoa powder
- 1¼ cups brown sugar
- 3 eggs
- 2 tsp vanilla essence
- ¼ tsp bicarb of soda
- ½ tsp sea salt flakes
- 1 cup all-purpose flour
- Handful hazelnuts (roasted, chopped)

Directions:

1. Preheat the main oven to 350 degrees F. Spritz an 8" square baking tin with nonstick spray, line with parchment and spritz again.

2. Using a double boiler, melt together the choc chips and unsalted butter. Stir until silky.

3. Mix in the cocoa powder.

4. Beat together the brown sugar, eggs, and vanilla essence in a separate bowl. Pour in the melted chocolate and mix until combined.

5. Fold in the bicarb of soda, sea salt flakes, and flour.

6. Pour the batter into the tin and sprinkle with the chopped nuts.

7. Place in the oven and bake for just over half an hour.

8. Allow to cool before cutting into portions.

Dark Stout Beer Brownies

Dark stout beer gives a more intense malty flavor to these already enticing brownies.

Portions: 12-14

Prep Time: 10mins

Cooking Time: 45mins

Total Time: 55mins

Ingredients:

- 1⅔ cup all-purpose flour flour
- 1 cup sweetened cocoa powder

- 1 tsp kosher salt
- ½ cup light brown sugar
- 2 cups white sugar
- 1 cup salted butter (melted)
- 4 medium eggs
- 1 tsp vanilla essence
- 1½ cups dark stout beer
- 1 cup semisweet choc chips

Directions:

1. Preheat the main oven to 350 degrees F. Line a 9" square baking tin with parchment.

2. Combine the flour, cocoa powder, and salt in a small bowl. Set to one side.

3. Beat together the sugars, melted butter, eggs, and vanilla using an electric stand mixer. With the mixer running slowly pour in the beer. Then add the flour mixture a little at a time.

4. When combined turn off the mixer and transfer half of the batter to the baking tin.

5. Sprinkle over the choc chips and then pour over the remaining batter.

6. Place in the oven and bake for 45 minutes.

7. Allow to cool before slicing.

Dulce De Leche Brownies

Dulce de leche is sweetened condensed milk that has been slowly cooked until richly golden and caramel. Delicious on its own, but out of this world when combined with a brownie.

Portions: 10-12

Prep Time: 10mins

Cooking Time: 40mins

Total Time: 50mins

Ingredients:

- Nonstick spray
- 6 ounces semisweet choc chips
- 8 tbsp. salted butter (chopped)
- ¼ cup Dutch cocoa powder
- 3 eggs

- 1 cup granulated sugar
- 1 tsp vanilla essence
- 1 cup plain flour
- 1 cup dulce de leche

Directions:

1. Preheat the main oven to 350 degrees F. Spritz an 8" square baking tin with nonstick spray, line with parchment and spritz again.

2. Using a double boiler, melt together the choc chips and butter. Stir until silky.

3. Take off the heat and immediately whisk in the cocoa powder. Allow to cool a little before beating in the eggs.

4. Beat in the sugar and vanilla essence, when combined, fold in the flour.

5. Transfer half of the batter to the baking tin.

6. Dollop a ⅓ of a cup of dulce de leche on top of the batter. Swirl with a knife.

7. Pour over the remaining brownie batter and then dollop the remaining dulce de leche on top. Again, swirl the dulce de leche with a knife.

8. Place in the oven and bake for approximately 40 minutes.

9. Allow to cool before slicing.

Fig and Walnut Brownies

Sophisticated fig and walnut brownies are the perfect grownup treat to serve with coffee.

Portions: 14-16

Prep Time: 10mins

Cooking Time: 35mins

Total Time: 45mins

Ingredients:

- Cooking spray
- 3 eggs
- 1¼ cups white sugar
- ¼ cup canola oil
- 1 tsp vanilla essence
- 1 ounce bitter choc chips (melted)
- 1 cup all-purpose flour
- ⅔ cup cocoa powder (unsweetened)
- ¼ tsp kosher salt
- ⅓ cup toasted walnuts (chopped)
- 1 cup dried figs (chopped)

Directions:

1. Preheat the main oven to 325 degrees F. Spritz an 8" square baking tin with cooking spray.

2. Beat together the eggs and white sugar. When combined whisk in the canola oil and vanilla essence.

3. Stir in the melted chocolate.

4. Fold in the flour, cocoa powder, and salt until incorporated.

5. Finally, stir in the walnuts and figs.

6. Pour the batter into the baking tin. Place in the oven and bake for just over half an hour.

7. Allow to cool before slicing.

Fudgy Greek Yogurt Brownies

Greek yogurt gives a creamy and light flavor to take the edge off the richness of these decadent fudgy brownies.

Portions: 12

Prep Time: 10mins

Cooking Time: 20mins

Total Time: 30mins

Ingredients:

- Nonstick spray

- ⅓ cup semisweet choc chips
- 1 tbsp. virgin coconut oil
- ½ cup sweetened cocoa powder
- ¾ cup white sugar
- ¼ cup light brown sugar
- ¾ cup all-purpose flour
- 1¼ cups plain full-fat Greek yogurt (at room temperature)
- 1 tsp pure vanilla essence
- ⅓ cup milk choc chips

Directions:

1. Preheat the main oven to 350 degrees F. Spritz an 8" square baking tin with nonstick spray.

2. Melt together the semisweet choc chips and coconut oil using a double boiler. Stir until silky and set aside to cool a little.

3. Whisk together the cocoa powder, white sugar, brown sugar, and flour in a medium bowl.

4. In a separate bowl, combine the Greek yogurt, vanilla essence, and cooled melted chocolate. Mix the flour mixture into the melted chocolate mixture a little at a time until just combined.

5. Pour the batter into the baking tin and scatter with the milk choc chips.

6. Place in the oven and bake for 20 minutes. Allow to cool and set before slicing and enjoying.

Gooey Milky Brownies

Chewy, moist brownies with a surprise ooey gooey milk center are just what the doctor ordered!

Portions: 14-16

Prep Time: 10mins

Cooking Time: 45mins

Total Time: 55mins

Ingredients:

- Nonstick spray

- 2 cups semisweet choc chips
- ¾ cup unsalted butter (chilled, chopped)
- 4 ounces bitter choc chips
- 3 eggs
- Yolk from 1 egg
- 1½ cups white sugar
- 1 tsp vanilla essence
- ¾ cup all-purpose flour
- ¼ tsp sea salt
- ¾ cup sweetened condensed milk

Directions:

1. Preheat the main oven to 350 degrees F. Cover an 8" square baking tin with aluminum foil and spritz with nonstick spray.

2. Melt together half of the semisweet chocolate with the butter and all of the bitter chocolate. Stir until silky. Beat in the eggs, yolk, sugar, and vanilla essence.

3. Fold in the flour and salt.

4. Transfer half of the brownie batter to the tin.

5. Place in the oven for 10 minutes.

6. Take out and sprinkle with the remaining semisweet choc chips. Spoon over the condensed milk.

7. Use the remaining brownie batter to pour over the milk in an even layer.

8. Pop back in the oven and cook for just over half an hour.

9. Allow to cool completely before chilling, then slicing.

Magic Mug Brownie

A single-serving brownie that can be whipped up in under five minutes with just a mug! Now that's what we call magic!

Portions: 1

Prep Time: 3mins

Cooking Time: 2mins

Total Time: 5mins

Ingredients:

- 1 tbsp. salted butter
- 2 tbsp. granulated sugar
- Yolk of 1 egg
- ¼ tsp vanilla essence
- 1 tbsp. sweetened cocoa powder
- 2 tbsp. plain flour
- ¼ tsp bicarb of soda
- Pinch kosher salt
- 2 tbsp. milk choc chips

Directions:

1. Add the butter and sugar to a large mug, pop in the microwave and cook until the mixture bubbles.

2. Take out and using a small whisk, add the egg yolk, vanilla, cocoa powder, flour, bicarb of soda, and kosher salt.

3. Stir in the milk choc chips.

4. Put back in the microwave and cook for 60-90 seconds on a 50% heat setting.

5. Enjoy!

Merlot Brownies

A healthy glug of full-bodied merlot gives these brownies an even richer and more decadent flavor.

Portions: 9

Prep Time: 10mins

Cooking Time: 55mins

Total Time: 1hour 5mins

Ingredients:

- 3 medium eggs
- 1 cup granulated sugar
- 1 tsp kosher salt
- ¼ cup salted butter (melted)
- ⅓ cup full-bodied merlot
- ½ cup all-purpose flour
- ½ cup sweetened cocoa powder
- ½ cup milk choc chips

Directions:

1. Preheat the main oven to 325 degrees F. Line a 9" square baking tin with parchment.

2. Beat the eggs, granulated sugar, kosher salt, melted butter, and merlot together in a mixing bowl.

3. Fold in the flour and cocoa powder until just incorporated.

4. Stir in the choc chips.

5. Pour the batter into the tin and place in the oven. Bake for just under an hour, until set.

6. Allow to cool before slicing and serving.

Mexican Spice Brownies

These tempting brownies get a taste of Mexico with cinnamon spice and a generous pinch of ground red pepper for a subtle fiery finish.

Portions: 12-14

Prep Time: 10mins

Cooking Time: 35mins

Total Time: 45mins

Ingredients:

- ⅓ tsp red pepper (ground)
- ½ cup plain flour
- 1½ tbsp. cinnamon
- 10 tbsp. unsalted butter
- ¼ tsp sea salt
- ¾ cup + 2 tbsp. cocoa powder (unsweetened)
- ½ tsp pure vanilla essence
- 2 eggs

Directions:

1. Preheat the main oven to 325 degrees F. Line an 8" square baking tin with parchment. Leave plenty of overhang.

2. Combine the red pepper, flour, and cinnamon in a bowl. Set to one side.

3. Melt together the butter, salt, and cocoa powder using a microwave. Allow to cool before whisking in the vanilla essence and eggs.

4. Fold the flour mixture into the chocolate mixture until combined.

5. Pour the batter into the tin and place in the oven. Bake for half an hour.

6. Allow to cool before lifting from the tin and slicing.

PB&B Brownies

PB&B? Peanut butter and banana of course! A winning combination and even better when in brownie form.

Portions: 8

Prep Time: 10mins

Cooking Time: 30mins

Total Time: 40mins

Ingredients:

- Butter (for greasing)
- Cocoa powder (for dusting)
- 2 overripe medium bananas (mashed)
- 1 cup granulated sugar
- 1 tsp vanilla essence
- ½ cup unsalted butter (melted)
- Pinch kosher salt
- ¾ cup plain flour

- ¼ cup unsweetened cocoa powder
- ½ cup organic smooth peanut butter (softened)

Directions:

1. Preheat the main oven to 350 degrees F. Grease a 9" square baking tin and dust with cocoa powder.

2. Combine the mashed banana, sugar, vanilla essence, and melted butter in a mixing bowl.

3. Fold in the kosher salt, flour, and cocoa powder. Pour the batter into the tin.

4. Dollop spoonfuls of peanut butter on top of the batter, use a knife to swirl.

5. Place in the oven and bake for just under half an hour.

6. Allow to cool and slice.

Pistachio Nut and Dark Chocolate Brownies

Luscious and smooth melted dark chocolate is the base for these divine brownies studded with roasted pistachio nuts.

Portions: 14-16

Prep Time: 10mins

Cooking Time: 35mins

Total Time: 45mins

Ingredients:

- 4 ounces 70% dark chocolate (chopped)
- 4 ounces unsalted butter
- 8 ounces white sugar
- 2 medium eggs
- 1 tsp baking powder
- 2 ounces plain flour

- Pinch salt
- 4 ounces pistachio nuts (roasted, chopped)

Directions:

1. Preheat the main oven to 355 degrees F. Line a 9" square baking tin with parchment.

2. Using a double boiler, melt together the chocolate and butter. Stir until silky.

3. Take off the heat and immediately whisk in the sugar. Allow to cool a little before beating in the eggs followed by the baking powder, flour, and salt.

4. Fold in the chopped nuts.

5. Transfer the batter to the baking tin.

6. Place in the oven and bake for half an hour.

7. Allow to cool a little before slicing and serving warm.

Red Velvet Truffled Brownies

These brownies are a truly indulgent combination of all our favorite things; red velvet cake, chocolate truffles, and cookies 'n crème biscuits!

Portions: 16-18

Prep Time: 15mins

Cooking Time: 20mins

Total Time: 2hours 35mins

Ingredients:

- Nonstick spray
- 1 cup salted butter (melted)
- 1 (18 ounce) box red velvet cake mix
- 2 medium eggs
- 35 cookies 'n crème biscuits
- 12 ounces semisweet choc chips
- 11½ ounces milk choc chips

- 1 cup heavy whipping cream

Directions:

1. Preheat the main oven to 350 degrees F. Line a 13x9" baking dish with aluminum foil and spritz with nonstick spray.

2. In a mixing bowl, beat together the melted butter, red velvet cake mix, and eggs until combined.

3. Transfer the mixture to the dish and bake in the oven for just over 15 minutes. Allow to cool a little.

4. Add the biscuits to a food processor and blitz until crumbed. Add the melted butter and blitz again until combined. Press the mixture evenly on top of the cake layer.

5. Add the semisweet choc chips to a bowl.

6. Bring the cream to a gentle boil in a saucepan and immediately pour over the semisweet choc chips. Allow to stand for a couple of minutes before stirring.

7. Pour the mixture over the biscuit layer.

8. Sprinkle with the milk choc chips before chilling for 1-2 hours.

9. Slice into squares and serve.

Salty Caramel Pretzel Brownies

These scrumptious brownies are a salty-sweet combination you won't want to miss.

Portions: 14-16

Prep Time: 10mins

Cooking Time: 35mins

Total Time: 45mins

Ingredients:

Pretzel Base:

- 1 cup pretzels (crushed)
- ½ cup all-purpose flour
- ½ cup light brown sugar
- ¼ tsp bicarb of soda
- ½ cup salted butter (melted)

Brownie:

- 7 ounces bitter choc chips
- ¾ cup salted butter
- ¼ cup water
- 1 cup light brown sugar
- ¾ cup white sugar
- 2 medium eggs
- 1 tsp vanilla essence
- 1⅓ cups all-purpose flour
- Pinch kosher salt
- Pinch cinnamon
- Topping:
- 2-3 ounces milk chocolate (melted)
- 12 caramel candies (melted)
- Sea salt flakes

Directions:

1. Preheat the main oven to 350 degrees F.

2. Combine the pretzels, flour, brown sugar, and bicarb of soda. Stir in the melted butter until combined. Press the mixture into the base of a large baking tin.

3. Place in the oven and bake for 10 minutes.

4. Melt together the choc chips, butter, and water in a saucepan over moderate heat. Stir until silky and take off the heat.

5. Whisk in the sugar, eggs, and vanilla essence. When combined, fold in the flour, salt, and cinnamon.

6. Pour over the baked crust layer.

7. Put back in the oven and bake for just under half an hour.

8. Allow to cool a little before drizzling over the melted chocolate and caramel. Sprinkle with sea salt flakes.

9. Slice and serve warm.

Strawberry Smash Brownies

Sweet fresh strawberries bring a fruity berry flavor to yummy brownies.

Portions: 14-16

Prep Time: 10mins

Cooking Time: 30mins

Total Time: 40mins

Ingredients:

- Nonstick spray
- 1½ ounces bitter chocolate
- ½ cup salted butter

- ½ cup cocoa powder (unsweetened)
- 1¼ white sugar
- ¼ tsp kosher salt
- 1 tsp vanilla essence
- 1 medium egg
- ¾ cup all-purpose flour
- 1 cup fresh strawberries (hulled, sliced)
- 8 ounces bittersweet choc chips

Directions:

1. Preheat the main oven to 350 degrees F. Spritz an 8" square baking tin with nonstick spray.

2. Melt together the bitter chocolate and butter in a saucepan over moderate heat. Stir until silky, take off the heat.

3. Immediately whisk in the cocoa powder, sugar, salt, vanilla essence, and egg until combined.

4. Fold in the flour.

5. Transfer the batter to the tin and place in the oven. Bake for just under half an hour.

6. Allow to cool before arranging the strawberries in a single neat layer on top.

7. Melt the choc chips using a double boiler and then drizzle over the strawberries.

8. Use a spatula to gently spread the chocolate out evenly, take care not to disturb the strawberry layer.

9. Chill until set and slice.

Triple Layered Coconut Brownies

A creamy coconut layer is sandwiched between moist, chewy brownie and rich chocolate ganache.

Portions: 16

Prep Time: 15mins

Cooking Time: 35mins

Total Time: 4hours 50mins

Ingredients:

- Butter (for greasing)
- Brownie Layer:
- 3 ounces semisweet choc chips
- ¾ cup salted butter
- 1 tsp granulated coffee
- 1 cup granulated sugar
- 3 medium eggs
- 1 tsp vanilla essence
- ¾ cup plain flour
- ½ tsp kosher salt
- 1 tbsp. cocoa powder

Coconut Layer:

- 1 (12 ounce) can sweetened condensed milk
- 2½ cups flaked coconut (unsweetened)

Ganache Layer:

- 4 ounces semisweet choc chips
- ½ cup heavy whipping cream

Directions:

1. Preheat the main oven to 350 degrees F. Grease an 8" square baking tin and line.

2. Melt together the choc chips and salted butter using a double boiler. Whisk until silky.

3. Take off the heat and stir in the granulated coffee and sugar. Allow to cool a little.

4. Beat in the eggs one at a time, then mix in the vanilla essence, flour, kosher salt, and cocoa powder.

5. Pour the batter into the tin and place in the oven for half an hour.

6. Allow to cool to room temperature before starting the coconut layer.

7. Stir together the condensed milk and flaked coconut. Spread the mixture in an even layer on top of the cooled brownie.

8. Then prepare the ganache. Place the choc chips in a bowl.

9. In a small saucepan over moderate heat warm the milk until begins to bubble at the edges. Immediately pour the cream over the choc chips and allow to stand for 60 seconds. Stir until silky.

10. Pour the ganache evenly over the coconut layer. Chill for 1-2 hours.

11. Slice into squares and serve!

Cream Cheese Brownies

Blackberry Cheesecake Topped Brownies

An irresistible combination of texture and flavor in every bite.

Portions: 9

Prep Time: 20mins

Cooking Time: 1hour 10mins

Total Time: 5hours 30mins

Ingredients:

Blackberry Puree:

- 6 ounces fresh or frozen blackberries
- ¼ cup granulated white sugar
- ¼ cup water

Brownies:

- ¾ cup unsalted butter
- 1½ cups sugar
- 2 medium eggs
- 2 tsp vanilla essence
- ½ tsp salt
- ¾ cup cocoa powder
- ½ cup all-purpose flour

Cheesecake:

- 8 ounces cream cheese, softened
- ¼ cup Greek yogurt
- 1 large egg (room temperature)
- ¼ cup sugar
- ½ tsp salt

Directions:

1. First, make the puree by combining the blackberries, white sugar, and water in a small pan over moderately high heat for between 8-10 minutes. Break down the berries using a spoon or whisk.

2. As soon as the berries are sufficiently cooked, strain over a mixing bowl and with a spatula, push through the berry liquid and discard any solids. Allow to cool to room temperature.

3. Preheat the main oven to 325 degrees F. Line an 8" square baking pan with parchment and put to one side.

4. In a microwave-safe bowl, in 20-second intervals, melt the butter. Add the sugar followed by the eggs, vanilla essence and salt and stir to combine.

5. Next, fold in the cocoa and flour and pour the batter into the pan, evenly spreading.

6. In an electric stand mixer, fitted with a whisk attachment, combine the cream cheese, yogurt, egg, sugar, and salt. Cream at moderately high speed for 2-3 minutes.

7. Pour the mixture over the batter, evenly spreading.

8. Drizzle with berry puree and using a knife or fork swirl into the cheesecake batter.

9. Bake in the oven for approximately an hour, or until the cheesecake is golden brown.

10. Transfer to the fridge for cool for 3-4 hours.

11. Slice and enjoy.

Cherry Garcia Brownies

These have to be the cherry on top of the cake! Simply the very best brownies ever.

Portions: 16 squares

Prep Time: 20mins

Cooking Time: 30mins

Total Time: 50mins

Ingredients:

Brownies:

- 1 cup butter (melted, cooled)
- 2½ cups granulated sugar
- 1 tbsp. vanilla essence
- 4 medium eggs
- 1½ cups wholewheat flour
- 1 cup cocoa
- ½ tsp salt

Cherry Cheesecake Filling:

- 1 (8 ounce) package cream cheese

- 1 medium egg
- 1 tsp vanilla essence
- ⅓ cup sugar
- ½ (21 ounce) can cherry pie filling

Directions:

1. Preheat the main oven to 350 degrees F. Line a 9x13" pan with aluminum foil.

2. For the brownies. In a large mixing bowl, whisk the butter with the sugar until silky. Add the vanilla essence and eggs, whisking until fully combined.

3. Next, add the flour, followed by the cocoa and salt, stirring to incorporate. The batter will be quite thick.

4. Spread, approximately half of the batter into the bottom of the prepared pan.

5. Make the filling: Using an electric mixer beat the cream cheese with the egg, vanilla essence and sugar until silky smooth.

6. Evenly spread the cream cheese mixture over the top of the brownie batter and top with spoonfuls of cherry pie filling, spreading a little.

7. With a spoon, drop the remaining batter over the top of the cherry pie filling, taking care to cover the whole surface, without attempting to spread it. Gently smooth out as best as you are able.

8. Bake in the oven, until the center when touched springs back; this will take around 30-35 minutes.

9. Allow to cool before slicing into squares.

Cinnamon Roll Breakfast Blondies

A freshly squeezed orange juice, a hot cup of coffee and a cinnamon roll blondie is the best way to start the day – every day.

Portions: 16

Prep Time: 20mins

Cooking Time: 25mins

Total Time: 45mins

Ingredients:

Blondies:

- ½ cup butter (melted)
- 1 cup brown sugar
- 1 medium egg
- 1½ tsp vanilla essence

- ¼ tsp salt
- 1 cup flour

Cinnamon Swirl:

- 1 tbsp. butter (melted)
- ¼ cup brown sugar
- 1 tsp cinnamon

Frosting:

- 4 ounces full-fat cream cheese (softened)
- ¼ cup butter (softened)
- ½ tsp vanilla essence
- 2 cups confectioner's sugar
- Milk
- Cinnamon (to serve)

Directions:

1. Preheat the main oven to 350 degrees F. Line an 8" square baking pan with aluminum foil.

2. To prepare the blondies: In a large mixing bowl, cream the melted butter with the brown sugar. Add the egg and vanilla essence and mix well until incorporated.

3. Add the salt followed by the flour and mix until silky smooth.

4. Evenly spread the mixture into the baking pan.

5. Next, make the filling: In a second bowl, combine the butter, along with the brown sugar and cinnamon. With a spoon drop dollops of the filling mixture over the surface of the blondie batter and with a blunt kitchen knife, gently swirl.

6. Bake in the oven for between 20-25 minutes.

7. Finally, make the frosting. In a medium-sized mixing bowl, combine the cream cheese with the butter, vanilla essence and confectioner's sugar. As soon as the ingredients are fully combined, whip until fluffy. Add a dash of milk to soften if necessary.

8. As soon as the blondies are sufficiently cool, frost and sprinkle with cinnamon.

German Chocolate Cream Cheese Brownies

Sometimes the traditional recipes are the best like these tried and trusted German brownies with a subtle hint of almond and sweet vanilla cream cheese filling.

Portions: 24

Prep Time: 15mins

Cooking Time: 40mins

Total Time: 2hours 55mins

Ingredients:

- Butter (for greasing)

Brownie:

- 4 ounces German sweet chocolate (roughly chopped)
- 3 tbsp. salted butter
- ¾ cup granulated sugar
- 1 tsp vanilla essence
- ¼ tsp almond essence
- 2 eggs

- ½ cup all-purpose flour
- ½ tsp baking powder
- ¼ tsp kosher salt
- ½ cup almonds (chopped)

Cream Cheese Filling:

- 3 ounces full-fat cream cheese (at room temperature)
- 1 egg
- ¼ cup granulated sugar
- 2 tbsp. salted butter (at room temperature)
- 1 tbsp. all-purpose flour
- ½ tsp vanilla essence

Directions:

1. Preheat the main oven to 325 degrees F. Grease an 8" square baking tin.

2. Using a double boiler, melt together the chocolate and butter. Stir until silky.

3. Take off the heat and immediately whisk in the sugar, essences, and eggs.

4. Fold in the flour, followed by the baking powder, salt, and chopped almonds.

5. Transfer half of the batter to the baking tin.

6. Beat together the cream cheese, egg, sugar, butter, flour, and vanilla. Spoon the mixture over the brownie batter in the pan. Swirl with a knife.

7. Pour the remaining brownie batter over the top.

8. Place in the oven and bake for just over 35 minutes.

9. Allow to cool before chilling for a couple of hours.

10. Slice and enjoy.

Hazelnut Brownies with Cream Cheese

Nut lovers will go crazy for these hazelnut brownies that are full of nutty flavor and texture.

Portions: 24

Prep Time: 25mins

Cooking Time: 35mins

Total Time: 1hour

Ingredients:
Filling:

- 3 ounces cream cheese (softened)
- ¼ cup granulated sugar
- 1 large egg
- 2 tsp freshly squeezed lemon juice
- ½ tsp vanilla essence
- ¼ cup hazelnuts (finely chopped)

Brownies:

- Butter (for greasing)
- ½ cup bittersweet chocolate chips
- 5 tbsp. unsalted butter
- 1 cup all-purpose flour
- ¼ tsp salt
- ¾ cup granulated sugar
- 2 large eggs
- 1 tsp vanilla essence
- ¾ cup hazelnuts (coarsely chopped)

Directions:

1. First, make the filling by beating the cream cheese with the sugar in a mixing bowl until silky smooth. Add the egg, freshly squeezed lemon juice and vanilla essences, beating until thoroughly blended. Add the nuts, stir to combine, cover the bowl and transfer to the fridge.

2. Next, make the brownies. Lightly grease a 9" square baking tin and set to one side.

3. In a pan, over the low heat, melt the chocolate chips along with the butter, while frequently stirring. Take the pan off the heat and then allow to cool.

4. Combine the flour with the salt and put to one side.

5. Beat the sugar with the eggs, add the vanilla essence along with the now cool chocolate mixture, beating until incorporated.

6. A little at a time, add the flour mixture, mixing until incorporated and stir in the hazelnuts.

7. Evenly spread 50 percent of the batter into the baking tin.

8. Carefully spread the chilled filling over the batter. Transfer to the fridge for 10 minutes.

9. Preheat the main oven to 350 degrees F.

10. Spread the remaining batter over the filling, this is a tricky process so take care.

11. Using a butter knife, swirl the layers.

12. Bake in the oven for just over half an hour. Allow to cool before slicing and serving.

Matcha Cream Cheese Brownies

Time for tea? Only if it's served with Green Tea Cream Cheese Brownies!

Portions: 16 squares

Prep Time: 15mins

Cooking Time: 45mins

Total Time: 55mins

Ingredients:

- Butter (for greasing)
- Green Tea Cream Cheese Batter:
- 4 ounces cream cheese (room temperature)
- ⅓ cup white sugar
- 1 medium egg (room temperature)
- 3 tbsp. heavy cream

- 1 tsp vanilla essence
- 1½ tsp matcha green tea powder
- 3 tbsp. all purpose flour
- ¼ tsp baking powder

Brownie Batter:

- 4 ounces dark chocolate (minimum 60%)
- ½ cup unsalted butter
- 1 cup white sugar
- 2 large eggs
- ⅓ cup all-purpose flour
- ½ tsp baking powder
- ¼ tsp kosher salt

Directions:

1. Preheat the main oven to 350 degrees F. Grease an 8" square baking tin and line with parchment.

2. Using an electric mixer fitted with a paddle beat the cream cheese with the sugar until lump free and smooth.

3. Beat in the egg and add the cream along with the vanilla essence.

4. Sift the Matcha Green Tea powder, flour, and baking powder into the batter and mix until incorporated. Put to one side.

5. Nest, make the brownie batter. In a double boiler, melt the chocolate.

6. In a mixing bowl, combine the melted chocolate with the sugar and eggs. Add the flour followed by the baking powder and salt, stir until fully combined.

7. Alternatively, spoon the Green Tea batter and the brownie batter into the baking pan.

8. Take a blunt knife and make a gentle swirling pattern, taking care not to blend the batters into each other.

9. Transfer to the preheated oven for 40-45 minutes.

10. Cool in the pan before cutting into even squares.

Mint Chocolate Low Carb Cheesecake Brownie Bars

With only 2.5g net carbs per square, you can afford to indulge your sweet tooth.

Portions: 16

Prep Time: 10mins

Cooking Time: 30mins

Total Time: 40mins

Ingredients:

Brownie layer:

- ¼ cup salted butter
- ¼ cup low-calorie sweetener
- ¾ cups almond flour
- 2 medium eggs
- 2 tbsp. unsweetened cocoa powder
- 2 tbsp. water

Cheesecake layer:

- 8 ounces low-fat cream cheese
- ¼ cup low-calorie sweetener
- 1 medium egg
- ½ tsp peppermint essence
- Green food gel

Directions:

1. Preheat the main oven to 350 degrees F. Using parchment paper line an 8" square pan.

2. In a stand mixer bowl, add the butter to the sweetener, and cream together.

3. Add the flour to the eggs, the cocoa powder, and water and beat until combined.

4. Transfer the mixture to the pan and bake in the oven for 10 minutes.

5. In the meantime, prepare the cheesecake layer: Beat together, until combined the cream cheese with the low-calorie sweetener, egg, and peppermint essence. Add the green food gel, a few drops at a time, until you achieve your desired shade.

6. As soon as the brownie layer has pre-baked, evenly spoon the cheesecake layer over the top and bake for another 20 minutes, or until the top layer is sufficiently baked through.

7. Allow to cool and cut into equal squares.

Mocha Brownies with Cream Cheese Coffee Frosting

The next time you want to impress at the bake sale or potluck, whip up these tantalizing mocha brownies with soft, fluffy coffee cream cheese frosting.

Portions: 14-16

Prep Time: 20mins

Cooking Time: 30mins

Total Time: 1hour 30mins

Ingredients:

Brownies:

- 4 ounces semisweet choc chips
- ½ cup unsalted butter
- 1 tbsp. coffee granules
- 2 eggs
- 1 cup white sugar
- 1 tsp vanilla essence
- ¾ cup + 2 tbsp. all-purpose flour
- ¼ tsp baking powder
- ½ tsp kosher salt

Frosting:

- 8 ounces full-fat cream cheese (softened)
- 4 tbsp. unsalted butter (softened)
- 2 tbsp. coffee granules (dissolved in 1 tbsp. hot water, cooled)
- ½ tsp vanilla essence
- 1½ cups confectioner's sugar

Directions:

1. Preheat the main oven to 350 degrees F. Line a 9" square baking tin with parchment.

2. Using a double boiler, melt together the chocolate and butter. Stir until silky.

3. Take off the heat and immediately whisk in the coffee granules.

4. Allow to cool before whisking in the eggs, sugar, and vanilla.

5. Fold in the flour, baking powder, and salt.

6. Transfer the batter to the tin and bake for just under half an hour. Allow to cool.

7. Prepare the frosting. Beat together the cream cheese, butter, coffee, and vanilla until combined.

8. Beat in the sugar a little at a time until you have a fluffy, spreadable frosting.

9. Frost the cooled brownies, slice and enjoy.

Orange Cream Cheese Chocolate Brownies

Chocolate and orange is the perfect marriage of flavors, and never more so than when put together in a brownie.

Portions: 18

Prep Time: 22mins

Cooking Time: 28mins

Total Time: 50mins

Ingredients:

- Cooking spray
- ⅔ cup all-purpose flour
- ½ tsp baking powder
- ½ tsp salt
- 4 ounces bittersweet chocolate (chopped)
- 2 ounces unsweetened chocolate (chopped)
- ½ cup + 2 tbsp. unsalted butter
- 1¼ cups sugar
- 2 tsp vanilla essence
- 3 large eggs

- 8 ounces full-fat cream cheese (room temperature)
- ⅔ cup powdered sugar
- 2 tbsp. unsalted butter (room temperature)
- 1½ tsp orange peel (finely grated)
- ½ cup toasted sweetened flaked coconut

Directions:

1. Set the oven rack in the lower middle part of the main oven and preheat to 325 degrees F. Lightly mist a 13x9" baking pan with cooking spray and press a large sheet of foil over the base and up the sides to make an overhang. Spray the foil with additional spray.

2. In a bowl, whisk the flour along with the baking powder and salt. Set to one side.

3. Heat the chocolates and the butter in a saucepan over moderately low heat, until it is melted and smooth and take the pan off the heat and stir until silky.

4. Whisk the sugar, vanilla essence, and eggs into the chocolate mixture, until smooth and glossy.

5. Add the set-aside dry ingredients and whisk until incorporated.

6. Pour the brownie batter into the baking pan and bake for 20-25 minute. Allow to cool.

7. With an electric mixer, beat the cream cheese, sugar, butter and orange peel in a bowl, until silky smooth.

8. Spread the frosting over the cooled brownie and sprinkle with toasted coconut.

9. Use the foil overhang to lift the brownies out of the pan.

10. Cut the brownies into squares and serve.

Pecan and Cranberry Brownie with Cream Cheese Swirls

Great texture and flavor combinations with these deliciously decadent brownies.

Portions: 9-12

Prep Time: 25mins

Cooking Time: 33mins

Total Time: 1hour 30mins

Ingredients:

- Butter (for greasing)
- 5⅓ ounces full-fat cream cheese

- 2 tbsp. whole milk
- 3½ ounces dark chocolate (roughly chopped)
- 3 tbsp. butter
- 3 ounces all-purpose flour
- ¼ tsp salt
- ½ tsp baking powder
- 1½ ounces unsweetened cocoa powder
- ¼ cup virgin olive oil
- 2 medium eggs
- 1 tbsp. instant coffee powder
- 1 cup brown sugar (tightly packed)
- 1 tsp vanilla essence
- ⅓ cup cream
- ¼ cup pecan nuts (roughly chopped)
- ¾ cup dried or fresh cranberries (divided)

Directions:

1. Preheat the main oven to 360 degrees F. Lightly grease then line an 8" square tin with parchment.

2. In a mixing bowl, mix the cream cheese along with the milk until silky smooth.

3. In a double boiler, melt the chocolate together with the butter, whisk to combine and put to one side.

4. In another bowl, sift the flour, salt, baking powder and cocoa powder together.

5. In a mixing bowl, beat together the virgin olive oil, eggs, coffee powder and sugar until silky smooth, this will take around 2-3 minutes. Add the vanilla essence followed by the cream, melted chocolate and mix thoroughly to combine.

6. Fold in the flour-cocoa mixture until incorporated, taking care not to over mix.

7. Fold in the pecans, along with ½ cup of cranberries.

8. Pour the brownie batter into the baking tin.

9. Using a spoon, add the cream cheese mixture haphazardly over the batter and using the back of the spoon, swirl.

10. Scatter the remaining cranberries over the top.

11. Bake in the preheated oven for 25-30 minutes.

12. Remove the pan from the oven and allow to cool.

13. Cut the brownies into equal squares and enjoy.

Peppermint Cream Cheese Brownies

A really scrummy after-dinner brownie to enjoy with a coffee.

Portions: 16

Prep Time: 20mins

Cooking Time: 35mins

Total Time: 55mins

Ingredients

Brownie:

- 5 ounces semisweet chocolate
- ½ cup butter
- 1 cup granulated sugar
- 2 medium eggs

- ¾ tsp peppermint extract
- ½ tsp vanilla essence
- ½ cup all-purpose flour
- 2 tbsp. dark chocolate cocoa powder
- ¼ tsp salt

Frosting:

- 4 ounces cream cheese (softened)
- ¼ cup butter (softened)
- 1¾ cups powdered sugar

Ganache:

- 3 tbsp. heavy whipping cream
- 1 ½ ounces bittersweet choc chips
- 1 candy cane (crushed)

Directions:

1. First, make the brownie. Preheat the main oven to 350 degrees F. Line an 8" square baking pan with parchment.

2. Add the chocolate and butter to a microwave-safe bowl and microwave in 25-second intervals until melted. Stir until smooth and silky.

3. Add the sugar followed by the eggs, peppermint extract, and vanilla essence.

4. Add the flour along with the cocoa powder, and salt and mix well until incorporated.

5. Transfer the mixture to the baking pan and bake for 30-35 minutes. Allow to cool.

6. Next, prepare the Frosting. In a bowl combine the cream cheese with the butter, beating together until silky smooth. Add the powdered sugar, stir to combine, and spread over the cooled brownies.

7. Finally, make the ganache. In a microwave-safe bowl, heat the cream in the microwave until it begins to boil. Add the chocolate

chips to the cream and cover the bowl for a couple of minutes, then whisk until lump-free and smooth.

8. Transfer the mixture to a piping bag and allow to cool for several minutes.

9. Pipe over the frosting and scatter with crushed candy canes.

10. Pull on the parchment paper to remove the brownie and then cut into evenly-sized squares.

Pink Velvet Swirl Cheesecake Brownies

Pretty pink cheesecake brownie squares make the perfect party nibbles.

Portions: 24

Prep Time: 15mins

Cooking Time: 25mins

Total Time: 4hours 15mins

Ingredients:

- Cooking spray
- 1 (15¼ ounce) box super moist cake mix
- ½ cup salted butter (melted)
- 1 medium egg
- 1 tsp chocolate extract
- 4 tbsp. whole milk
- 1 tsp hot pink food gel
- 8 ounces full-fat cream cheese (softened)
- ¼ cup sugar
- 1 medium egg
- 1 tsp vanilla essence

Directions:

1. First, prepare your ingredients.

2. Preheat the main oven to 325 degrees F. Using parchment, line a 9x13" baking pan, and lightly mist the foil with cooking spray.

3. In a bowl, combine the cake mix with the butter, followed by the egg, chocolate extract, 2 tbsp. whole milk and the pink gel. Stir well to combine.

4. Put ½ cup of pink batter to one side, and pour the rest into the baking pan.

5. Add the remaining milk to the ½ cup of pink batter, to thin it.

6. In a processor, pulse the cream cheese together with the sugar. Add the egg followed by the vanilla essence, and stir to combine.

7. Pour the mixture over the batter.

8. Drizzle the pink batter set aside earlier over the cheesecake and using a fork, make swirling patterns.

9. Bake in the oven for 17 minutes.

10. Remove the pan from the oven and cover with aluminum foil.

11. Return to the oven for 6-8 minutes.

12. Allow to cool for half an hour before transferring to the fridge for 2-3 hours.

13. When you are ready to serve, cut into squares.

Pumpkin Cheesecake Brownie Swirls

You don't have to wait until fall to make these scrumptious swirls.

Portions: 24-30

Prep Time: 10mins

Cooking Time: 30mins

Total Time: 40mins

Ingredients:

- 2 (21 ounce) boxes brownie mix
- 1 (17¾ ounce) box pumpkin cheesecake mix
- 8 ounces cream cheese (room temperature)

Directions:

1. Preheat the main oven to 350 degrees F.

2. In a large mixing bowl, mix the brownie batter according to the package directions using all extra ingredients called for. Divide the mixture between 2 (9x13") pans.

3. In a second bowl, combine the cheesecake box's spice mix with the cream cheese and follow the package directions, using either a stand or hand mixer.

4. Add the pumpkin from the pumpkin cheesecake box and stir in until just combined, as this will prevent it from being chalky.

5. Using a spoon, dollop the cheesecake mix into the brownie pans.

6. Swirl a butter knife, through the brownie pans at various angles to make an attractive pattern.

7. Bake for just under half an hour.

8. Allow to cool, then slice and enjoy.

Salted Caramel & Apple Cheesecake Brownie Squares

Apple cheesecake brownie squares drizzled with salted caramel sauce are perfect to come home to after a hard day.

Portions: 16

Prep Time: 20mins

Cooking Time: 35mins

Total Time: 1hour 25mins

Ingredients:

- Nonstick Spray

Brownies:

- ¾ cup all-purpose flour
- ¼ cup unsweetened cocoa powder

- ⅛ tsp salt
- ½ cup unsalted butter (room temperature)
- ½ cup white sugar
- 2 medium eggs
- 1 tsp vanilla essence

For the cheesecake:

- 8 ounces cream cheese (softened)
- 1 large egg
- ¼ cup white sugar
- ½ tsp vanilla essence
- Apples:
- 1½ cups apple (peeled, cored, chopped small)
- ⅓ cup pecans (chopped)
- ¼ tsp nutmeg
- 1 tsp cinnamon

Topping:

- Salted caramel sauce

Directions:

1. Preheat the main oven to 355 degrees F and line an 8" square baking tin with aluminum foil, making sure you leave an overhang. Lightly mist the foil with nonstick spray and set to one side.

2. First, make the brownies. In a mixing bowl, combine the flour with the cocoa powder and salt and set to one side.

3. In a bowl, cream the butter and white sugar until fluffy. One at a time, add the eggs.

4. Add the vanilla essence and slowly combine the flour mixture with the wet ingredients, mixing until incorporated. Take care not to over-mix.

5. Pour the batter into the baking tin. Set to one side.

6. For the cheesecake; in the bowl of an electric mixer on moderate speed, beat the softened cream cheese with the large egg,

granulated sugar, and vanilla essence, until completely combined and smooth, remembering to scrape the side of the bowl as needed.

7. Evenly spread the mixture over the brownie and set to one side.

8. In a medium-sized bowl, toss the apples with the chopped pecans, nutmeg, and cinnamon. Scatter the apple mixture over the cream cheese and gently but firmly press down so that they stick to one another.

9. Bake in the oven for 35-40 minutes, or until set. Allow to cool for half an hour before transferring to the fridge to chill.

10. Cut into even squares and drizzle with salted caramel topping.

Tipsy Brownies with Irish Cream Liqueur

An adult-only brownie to enjoy all year round.

Portions: 20

Prep Time: 1hour 40mins

Cooking Time: 55mins

Total Time: 2hours 5mins

Directions:

- Nonstick spray
- 1½ cups all-purpose flour
- ½ tsp bicarb of soda
- ½ tsp kosher salt
- 12 tbsp. unsalted butter
- 1 cup granulated sugar
- ¼ cup cold water
- 1 cup semisweet choc chips
- 1 cup unsweetened baking chocolate (finely chopped)
- 2 tsp vanilla essence

- 1½ tsp instant espresso powder
- 4 medium eggs

Cream cheese layer:

- 16 ounces cream cheese (softened)
- 1 medium egg
- ⅓ cup granulated sugar
- 1 tsp vanilla essence
- ¼ cup Irish cream liqueur

Directions:

1. Preheat the main oven to 350 degrees F. Using parchment paper line a 9x13" baking tin, lightly mist with nonstick spray.

2. First, make the brownie batter. In a bowl, whisk the flour together with the bicarb of soda and salt.

3. Add the butter, followed by the sugar and water to a pan, and over moderately high heat, boil. When boiling, immediately take off the heat.

4. Whisk in the choc chips, chopped baking chocolate, vanilla essence and instant espresso, stirring until the chocolate melts. One at a time, add the eggs, whisking thoroughly between each addition.

5. Slowly whisk in the flour mixture, whisking until the mixture is combined and smooth.

6. Finally, make the cream cheese layer by placing the cream cheese, egg, granulated sugar, vanilla essence, and Irish cream liqueur in a bowl, and using an electric mixer on moderate speed, beat until smooth, this will take around 3-4 minutes.

7. Pour approximately half the batter into the prepared pan and evenly spread.

8. Using a spoon, add the cream cheese mixture to the top of the brownie batter, and using a blunt knife, carefully distribute over the top.

9. Pour the remaining brownie batter over the top of the cream cheese and evenly spread.

10. Transfer to the preheated oven and bake for between 45-50 minutes.

11. Allow to completely cool before slicing into bars.

Tiramisu Brownies

The classic Italian dessert reinvented as a pop in the mouth brownie.

Portions: 24 brownies

Prep Time: 20mins

Cooking Time: 25mins

Total Time: 45mins

Ingredients:

- 1 (18.3 ounce) family size brownie mix*
- 4 tbsp. instant coffee
- ½ cup whole milk
- 1 (3½ ounce) box cheesecake pudding mix
- 1 (8 ounce) package cream cheese (softened)
- 1 (16 ounce) container cool whip (thawed, divided)

- ½ cup hot water
- 2½ cups lady finger cookies (broken into chunks)
- Cocoa powder

Directions:

1. First, bake the brownies according to the package instructions and allow to cool.

2. Dissolve 2 tablespoons of instant coffee in the whole milk.

3. Whisk in the cheesecake mix and put to one side.

4. In a mixing bowl, beat the cream cheese until fluffy. Fold in the cheesecake pudding/coffee mixture along with half of the cool whip.

5. Dissolve the remaining coffee in the water, stir to combine and drizzle over the ladyfinger cookie chunks.

6. Spread approximately half of the pudding mix over the cool brownies.

7. Arrange the ladyfinger cookie chunks on top of the pudding and cover with the reaming pudding mixture.

8. Top with cool whip and lightly dust with cocoa.

9. Transfer to the refrigerator until you are ready to serve.

Triple Decker Crunch Brownies

These impressively tall brownies are a mouth-watering stack of brownie, cheesecake, and chocolate peanut butter puff rice crunch.

Portions: 16-18

Prep Time: 20mins

Cooking Time: 35mins

Total Time: 3hours 55mins

Ingredients:

- Nonstick spray

Brownie:

- 6 tbsp. salted butter
- ¼ cup cocoa powder (unsweetened)
- 6 ounces semisweet choc chips
- ¼ tsp baking powder
- ¾ cup all-purpose flour
- ¼ tsp kosher salt
- 1 cup white sugar
- 2 tsp vanilla essence
- 2 medium eggs

Cheesecake:

- 2 (8 ounce) packages full-fat cream cheese
- 2 medium eggs
- ¼ cup white sugar
- 2 tbsp. plain flour
- 2 tbsp. whole milk
- 1 tsp vanilla essence

Puff Rice:

- 1 cup smooth organic peanut butter
- 1 cup semisweet choc chips
- ½ cup chocolate hazelnut spread
- 3 cups puffed rice cereal

Directions:

1. Preheat the main oven to 350 degrees F. Line a 9x13" baking tin with parchment and spritz with nonstick spray.

2. First, make the brownie. Using a double boiler, melt together the butter, cocoa powder, and choc chips. Stir until silky and take off the heat. Allow to cool a little.

3. In a small bowl, combine the baking powder, flour, and salt. Set to one side.

4. Using an electric whisk, beat together the sugar, vanilla, and eggs. With your whisk still running add the melted chocolate. When combined fold in the flour mixture until incorporated.

5. Transfer to the baking tin and smooth the surface with the back of a spoon or spatula.

6. Place in the oven and bake for 15 minutes.

7. Next, make the cheesecake. Beat together the cream cheese, eggs, sugar, flour, milk, and vanilla using an electric whisk. Spoon on top of the half-cooked brownie layer. Again, smooth surface.

8. Put back in the oven and bake for just over 15 minutes. Allow to completely cool.

9. Finally, prepare the puff rice crunch.

10. Melt together the peanut butter, choc chips, and hazelnut spread in a large saucepan over moderate heat. Stir until silky.

11. Take off the heat and stir in the puff rice cereal until combined and coated.

12. Press the puff rice mixture gently on top of the cheesecake layer.

13. Chill for 2-3 hours before slicing and enjoying.

Tropical Mango Brownies

Enjoy a taste of the Caribbean with these decadent mango brownies.

Portions: 32

Prep Time: 15mins

Cooking Time: 37mins

Total Time: 1hour 20mins

Ingredients:

- Nonstick spray
- 4 ounces unsweetened chocolate (chopped)
- ¾ cup butter
- 2 cups sugar
- 5 medium eggs
- 1½ cups + 2 tbsp. flour
- 1 package cream cheese (softened)
- 2 tsp ground cardamom
- 1 cup canned sweeten mango pulp

Directions:

1. Preheat the main oven to 350 degrees F. Spritz a 9x13" baking tin with non-stick spray.

2. In a microwave-safe bowl, on a medium setting, melt the chocolate along with the butter. Stir until the chocolate is melted and the mixture is incorporated.

3. Stir in 1½ cups of sugar and one at a time add the eggs, mixing well with each addition.

4. Add 1½ cups of flour until just combined. Pour the batter into the tin.

5. In a bowl, using an electric mixer beat the cream cheese with the remaining flour and cardamom, mix until incorporated.

6. Add the mango pulp, mixing well to combine.

7. Beat in the remaining egg until incorporated.

8. Using a spoon, drop the cream cheese mixture on top of the brownie batter and with a blunt knife gently swirl.

9. Bake in the oven for just over half an hour.

10. Allow to cool, slice into squares and serve.

White Russian Brownies

One for the adults; luscious fudgy brownies flavored with a generous glug of coffee liqueur and vodka, just like the famous White Russian cocktail.

Portions: 12

Prep Time: 15mins

Cooking Time: 40mins

Total Time: 1hour 55mins

Ingredients:

Brownie:

- 1¼ cups granulated sugar

- 4 tbsp. salted butter (at room temperature)
- 2 medium eggs
- ½ cup coffee liqueur
- ¼ tsp baking powder
- 1 cup flour
- ½ cup cocoa powder (unsweetened)
- ¼ tsp kosher salt

Vodka Cream Cheese:

- ¼ cup granulated sugar
- ¼ cups all-purpose flour
- ½ pound full-fat cream cheese (at room temperature)
- 1 medium egg
- 2 tbsp. salted butter (at room temperature)
- ¼ cup good quality vodka
- ¼ cup coffee flavor liqueur (for brushing)

Directions:

1. Preheat the main oven to 325 degrees F. Line a 9" square baking pan with parchment.

2. First, make the brownie batter. Beat together the granulated sugar, and butter. Beat in the eggs, followed by ½ cup coffee liqueur. When combined, fold in the baking powder, flour, cocoa powder, and salt.

3. Pour half of the mixture into the baking pan.

4. Next prepare the vodka cream cheese. Beat together the sugar, flour, cream cheese, egg, and butter. When combined, stir in the vodka. Spread on top of the brownie batter evenly.

5. Pour over the remaining batter.

6. Place in the oven and bake for approximately 40 minutes.

7. Allow to cool a little. While still warm, brush the top of the brownie with coffee liqueur.

8. Set aside for an hour before slicing and serving.

Zucchini Cream Cheese Frosted Brownies

Zucchini is a great addition to any cake, not only does it help to keep the cake moist but it's really low in calories too.

Portions: 16-18

Prep Time: 20mins

Cooking Time: 35mins

Total Time: 1hour 25mins

Ingredients:

Brownies

- 1½ cups all-purpose flour
- 1 tsp bicarb of soda
- ¾ tsp baking powder
- ½ tsp salt
- 2 medium eggs
- 1½ cups sugar
- ¾ cup vegetable oil

- 2 ounces of unsweetened chocolate (melted, cooled)
- 1½ cups zucchini (finely grated)
- ½ cup nuts (finely chopped)

Cream Cheese Frosting:

- 6 ounces cream cheese
- 6 tbsp. butter
- 1½ tsp vanilla
- 3½-4 cups confectioner's sugar

Directions:

1. For the brownies: In a mixing bowl, combine the flour, bicarb of soda, salt, baking powder. Set aside.

2. Add the sugar, vegetable oil and melted chocolate to an electric mixer and beat until incorporated.

3. With the mixer running, beat in the set-aside flour mixture a little at a time until incorporated.

4. With a spoon, stir in the shredded zucchini and nuts.

5. Transfer the batter to a lightly greased and floured baking pan, preferably 15x10" in size.

6. Bake in the oven on 350 degrees F. for just over half an hour. Allow to cool.

7. In the meantime, make the frosting. In a bowl, using an electric mixer beat the cream cheese with the butter and vanilla, until fluffy.

8. A little at a time, beat in the confectioner's sugar until the mixture is spreadable.

9. Spread the mixture over the brownie in the pan, slice into equal portions and serve.

Author's Afterthoughts

Thanks ever so much to each of my cherished readers for investing the time to read this book!

I know you could have picked from many other books but you chose this one. So a big thanks for downloading this book and reading all the way to the end.

If you enjoyed this book or received value from it, I'd like to ask you for a favor. Please take a few minutes to post an honest and heartfelt review on Amazon.com. Your support does make a difference and helps to benefit other people.

Thanks!

Printed in Great Britain
by Amazon

32266281R00071